S0-EKA-311

DISCARD

Unicorn French Series / Queneau

Unicorn French Series

Unicorn French Series

Raymond Queneau

TRANSLATED FROM THE FRENCH

BY

TEO SAVORY

1971

Unicorn Press

WITHDRAWN
Pierce Library
Eastern Oregon University
1410 L Avenue
La Grande, OR 97850

Translation and Introduction Copyright © 1971 by
Teo Savory
By arrangement with Editions Gallimard, Paris
Copyright © 1952

*This book is volume eleven in the Unicorn
French Series: Teo Savory, editor*

Designed by Alan Brilliant, printed by Elmer Pickard
Linotype composition by Achilles Friedrich
Bindery by Gordon Thomsen and Patricia Field
All rights reserved
Published by Unicorn Press
P.O. Box 1469
Santa Barbara, California 93102, U.S.A.

Some of these translations have appeared in *Works,
The Notebooks of Pierre Menard, Contemporary
Literature in Translation.* A grant was received from
the National Endowment for the Arts during the time
this book was being published.

*L.C. Catalogue Number 69-13017
S.B.N. 0-87775-004-1*

CONTENTS

RAYMOND QUENEAU, *surrealist, poet, mathematician, novelist, co-founder of* The Institute of 'Pataphysics, *essayist, editor of* Editions Pleiades, *black humorist, linguistic innovator, is too little known in English. His film,* Zazie dans le Métro, *has been shown in the United States, a few of his stylistically unique novels have been translated, as well as his linguistic tour de force,* Exercises in Style *(Gaberbocchus, London), but Americans have been deprived of the delightful and unsettling rewards of his poetry. The Unicorn French Series attempts to remedy this lack in its eleventh bi-lingual publication. Included are excerpts from Queneau's sequence,* Pour un art poétique, *in which he is anti-poet, and displays his total dislike of all shibboleths and pomposity.*

ON TRANSLATING QUENEAU

A glance at Queneau's poems might lead to a superficial labeling of their content as humor — sometimes light, sometimes black. This would be superficial indeed. What has been overlooked in the English-speaking world as much as his poetry itself is Queneau's linguistic influence, one quite as profound in our times as that of Joyce. Because his experiments with language, his innovations, take the form of surrealistic — 'pataphysical — humor, this influence on contemporary language and contemporary French writing may not be given the importance that is its due. (A comparison with the early position of Shaw, docketed by some of his critics, no matter how serious his themes, as a "humorist," comes to mind here.)

As for translating Queneau's poetry, there are of course many difficulties. Before even attempting to translate him, his poems must first be read aloud. Take the "untranslatable" poem, *Les Ziaux.* Even the title defies us, for he has combined the words "waters" (here translated as "seas") and "eyes" into a single word, adding to our difficulties by giving the result a phonetic spelling. A great deal of his desired effect he obtains by rhyming. Queneau cannot be translated unless one understands why he rhymes; it is not because he is "old-fashioned" or wants to use old forms, but because it is one of the ways he uses to play about with language. And, note well, he rhymes for sound rather than sense. (But to the ear, all that he expresses is sense.) Thus the translator must cope with and supply these end-rhymes; otherwise, forget this important and fascinating poet and turn to something easy, such as Ponge or prose (not Queneau's prose, though). However, end-rhymes are the least of our difficulties: many of Queneau's poems contain a complexity of interior rhyme and assonance, of plays on *made-up* words and phonetic innovations. Take, for instance, again in *Les Ziaux*, "nuitent le jour, jurent la nuit," in which we have a made-up word, "nuitent," followed closely by the word "jurent," used only for its playful proximity to "jour . . . " Then, after the rather successful translation of this phrase, the translator sacrifices "chants de dimanche à samedi," with its unusual rhyming of "samedi" with "nuit," in order to produce an end-rhyme for "night" and lets us down with "singing from dusk to daylight" — being faced with the greater problem of giving at least an approximation of the sound of the several matching end-rhymes the author has used more or less throughout the poem.

As Queneau is not literal-minded himself, and as literal translations of his poems utterly destroy their essence, the translator must try, as far as possible, to enter into the poet's own spirit and render the poem in *his* way. Of course, as one is not this unique spirit, "q-u-e-n-e-a-/u-r-a-i- grec mond" (*Viellir*), the translation will always fall short and be only an "almost-nearest poem."

7

LES ZIAUX

les eaux bruns, les eaux noirs, les eaux de merveille
les eaux de mer, d'océan, les eaux d'étincelles
nuitent le jour, jurent la nuit
chants de dimanche à samedi

les yeux vertes, les yeux bleues, les yeux de succelle
les yeux de passante au cours de la vie
les yeux noires, yeux d'estanchelle
silencent les mots, ouatent le bruit

eau de ces yeux penché sur tout miroir
gouttes secrets au bord des veilles
tout miroir, toute veille en ces ziaux bleues ou vertes
les ziaux bruns, les ziaux noirs, les ziaux de merveille

THE SEYES

brown seas, black seas, seas of marvel
seas of springs, seas of salt, seas of sparkle
they night the day and daze the night
singing from dusk to daylight

green eyes, blue eyes, eyes of marble
eyes of passing women throughout life
dark eyes, eyes of periwinkle
they silence words and muffle strife

seas of eyes poring over every mirror
secret droplets edging every vigil
every mirror, every vigil in green-blue seas-eyes
sighs of brown, sighs of black, sighs of marvel

8

HIPPOCAMPS

Green hippocamps
swimmers in odd streams
you populate
my winter dreams

I prefer you to
Pegasus or unicorn
you of heavy tread
and tick-infested horn

All passers-by avoid
the reverberating drum
of hoofs which hides
your deathlike boredom

SINES

When One made love to Zero
spheres embraced their arches
and prime numbers caught their breath
holding out their hands to fresh larches
simple fractions   fractured to death
lay down in the torrent of silent decimals

When B made love to A
the paragraphs caught fire
the commas caught their breath
holding their necks over a bridge's arc
and the alphabet   fractured to death
vanished into the arms of a silent question-mark

IF YOU THINK FOR ONE MINUTE

If you think for one minute
my girl
if you think that
this that this that this'll
go on forever
this season of
season of love
then whistle my girl
whistle girl in the wind

If you think girl
if you think ah
think your rosepetal skin
your little waspwaist
your dimpled chin
your nymphlike thigh
your delicate ankle
and downy arms
If you think girl
that this that this'll
go on forever
then whistle my girl
whistle girl in the wind

Fine days will pass
fine days on the grass
or the beach   soon
out of reach   the suns
and their planets
turn in their orbits
but you my girl
you go straight on
toward what you don't see
approaching so slyly
the quick wrinkle
the ruined dimple
the thick ankles and waist
so gather   gather you
rosebuds while you may
roses of life
and let their petals be
your wide sea of pleasure
If you don't my girl
if you don't then whistle
my girl in the wind

POOR FELLOW

Toto has a goat's nose and the foot of a pig
He carries his socks
in a matchbox
and he combs his hair
with a hung-up paper-cutter
If he gets dressed the walls turn grey
If he gets up the bed explodes
If he washes the water snorts
In his button-hole
he always has a button-hook

Poor fellow

TOWARD A POETIC ART

I

A poem's just a little thing
Hardly more than a cyclone in the Antilles
a typhoon in the China Seas
an earthquake in Nanking

A flood in the Yang-tse Kiang
at one fell swoop drowns you a thousand Chinese
bang
that's not even the subject for a poem
Nothing much

We keep busy in our village
going to build a better school
going to vote for a new mayor
    and change our market days

we used to be the hub of the universe but now
    we find we're near the ocean current that
    the horizon gnaws at

A poem's just a little thing

Toward a Poetic Art

III

Well placed well chosen
some words to make a poem
words . . . it's enough to love 'em
in order to write a po-em
we don't always know what we're saying
when the poem's little
we have to go back and look for the theme
to give a title
to our poeme
other times we laugh or cry
while writing poetry
it's always sumpn extreme
a poem

Toward a Poetic Art

V

Good lord good lord I want to write a little poem
Hold on here's one right now passing by
Come on little one
here where I can lead you
snap your lead onto the collar of my other poems
here where I can encase you
into the compression of my complete works
where I can enpaper you
and enrhyme you
enrhythm you
enlyric you
enpegasus you
enverse you
enprose you

oh the bitch
    she's shoved off

TOWARD A POETIC ART

VI

Black inkwell moonlight
black inkwell moonlight
moonlight black inkwell
moonlight black inkwell
poor poet's pen's ready
poor poet's pen's ready
it's a little cooler tonight
black inkwell moonlight
pen's run over white paper

pen's tracked some little black tracks
white moon dark inkwell they're
this newborn's father and mother
white moon dark inkwell

TOWARD A POETIC ART

VII

When poets are bored then they o-
Ften decide to pick up a pen and write a po-
Em   You understand that these conditions so-
Metimes tickle up a little poetry po-
Etry

Toward a Poetic Art

VIII

Where's my pome-ledger
now that I need it
no paper no pen
less poem
and here I am faced with nothing
nothing at all
nothingness
oh if only I could feel metaphysical
without fire or candle
and be poetical

Pierce Library
Eastern Oregon University
1410 L Avenue
La Grande, OR 97850

Toward a Poetic Art

IX

This evening
what if I were writing a poem
for posterity?

the hell with
that splendid idea

I feel sure of myself
I'll go ahead
and

to posterity
I'll say shit and doubleshit
and doubledoubleshit

cleverly tricking
that posterity
waiting for its poem

yes but

Toward a Poetic Art

XI

A train whistling in the night
'S a subject for poetic flight
A train whistling in Rome
'S a subject for a pome

A train whistling melod-
Iously's a subject for an ode
A train whistling like a linnet
'S a subject for a sonnet

And a train whistling like a ground-hog
Can make a rhymed prologue
But only a train whistling in the night
'S a fit subject for poetic flight

"Wise fox . . . "

Wise fox his eyes are subtle
sinuous snake grass is fertile
trumps of flowers in the meadow
birds wending between leaves
harsh sun water smiles in shadow
the hen shakes her sleeves . . .
. . . .

. . . and feathers fly oh subtle
fox now snicked by the agile
snare: then the trampled-under
grass gathers mingled blood
of scarlet-throated bird
and the murdered hunter

THE HUMAN SPECIES

The human species has given me
the right to be mortal
the duty to be civilized
a conscience
2 eyes that don't always function very well
a nose in the middle of my face
2 feet 2 hands
speech

the human species has given me
my father and mother
some brothers maybe who knows
a whole mess of cousins
and some great-grandfathers
the human species has given me
its 3 faculties
feeling intellect and will
each in moderation
32 teeth and 10 fingers a liver
a heart and some other viscera
the human species has given me
what I'm supposed to be satisfied with

THE DOGS OF ASNIÈRES

We bury dogs we bury cats
we bury horses we bury men
we bury hope we bury life
we bury love — lovers
we bury lovers — love
we bury silence
we bury peace in peace
peace — deepest peace
under a bed of fine multicolored gravel
of scallop shells and multicolored flowers

there's a tomb for everyone
on a lay-away plan
it's night it's day
on a lay-away plan

the Seine descends to the sea
the immovable island does not descend
the Seine will climb back to its source
on a lay-away plan
and the island will sail to the seaport
on a lay-away plan

we bury dogs we bury cats
two species who don't get along together

APPROXIMATIONS

To the almostnearest swan
the ducklings sing
to the almostnearest pine
two bellwethers ring

To the almostnearest donkey
a curate stirs
to the almostnearest peacock
a beetle whirs

To the almostnearest alder
some onions proudly sprout
to the almostnearest person
is passed the shit that's all about

To the almostnearest poem
the catgut scrapers mewl & purr
the catgut scraper critics
with the tick-ticks in their furr

THE HAPPY TINKER

Who knows if you'll die
said the tinker
basting the hole in the round casserole
It may be a lie
from the brain
of some thinker
and you'll never have to worry again

The tin flows past the bus-stop
along the cracked sidewalk
it's raining in his shop
its walls are cheese and chalk

I think
this tink-
er's saying death has lost its sting
He's too tact-
ful in fact
to say that dust's the end of everything

Who knows if you'll die
said the tinker
basting the hole in the round casserole
It may be a lie
from the brain
of some thinker
and you'll never have to worry again

IDEAS

Birds that are blue in the air are green in the grassland
who hears them sees them who sees them hears them
their expanded wings widen their homeland
but always through their feathers a fire spreads

Nimble chameleons of the sky that our eyes transpierce
living clouds little by little assume in turn
an idea's form and then the same one in reverse
proteans whose heavens do not limit any turn

They fly through the sublime excellence
of divine principles stamped on the horizon
sometimes the stars denote their presence
and the moon's games in the course of a season

SHADOW OF A DOUBT

I'm asking I'm asking what's going go-
ing on under this bowl of indigo
you say it that way so it'll rhyme
and there's no doubt at this time
the whole bloody world's all screw
'd up in a great big pot of stew

We're like a lot of half-wits here
on this round naturallyenough sphere
it's hard to find a word strong enough
for this agony if you bluff
your way through it till it's over
and you can *requiescat in pace* or clover

People go right left or middle
as if the whole thing wasn't a riddle
well that's life, that is, everywhere
and it's death certainly and burials
that cause all these funerals
that you see here and there

A MILLION FACTS

On my table lies an almanac from Hachette
for the year 1922. I had to get
it priced at four francs this omnium gatherum
that's seldom found bound in vellum
or Russian leather. One day feeling practical
I had to learn a now-admitted statistical
fact concerning the culture and disease
of opium imposed by the English on the Chinese
This work presents itself to the eye in a form
I find agreeable: neither too light nor too enorm-
ous. It has more than two hundred pages in half-
quarto and less than three hundred; bound in limp calf.
It's documentary and never takes one side
over another. Its erudition is world-wide
If you want to know the name of the Japan-
ese Minister of Sports you have only to scan
the proper page of this good book. This information
ascertained you can turn your whole attention
to the account of the diplomatic tension
between the USSR and the Balkans. But nowhere
does the geologic section state that volcanic
rocks (as I recall) are truffled into the soil there
So now I'm quite disgusted with my Almanic

TABLE

HIPPOCAMPES

Hippocampes verts
nageurs singuliers
vous avez peuplé
mes rêves d'hiver

Autant préférer
Pégase! Licorne!
pou d'ivoire gris
qui trotte paisible

Le passant s'enfuit
loin du réverbère
sous lequel enfoui
un mort désespère

CYGNES

Quand Un fit l'amour avec Zéro
Les sphères embrassèrent les tores
Et les nombres premiers s'avancèrent
Tendant leurs mains vers les frais sycomores
Et les fractions continues blessées à mort
Dans le torrent des décimales muettes se couchèrent

Quand B fit l'amour avec A
Les paragraphes s'embrasèrent
Les virgules s'avancèrent
Tendant leur cou par-dessus les ponts de fer
Et l'alphabet blessé za mort
S'évanouit dans les bras d'une interrogation muette

SI TU T'IMAGINES

Si tu t'imagines
si tu t'imagines
fillette fillette
si tu t'imagines
xa va xa va xa
va durer toujours
la saison des za
la saison des za
saison des amours
ce que tu te goures
fillette fillette
ce que tu te goures

Si tu crois petite
si tu crois ah ah
que ton teint de rose
ta taille de guêpe
tes mignons biceps
tes ongles d'émail
ta cuisse de nymphe
et ton pied léger
si tu crois petite
xa va xa va xa
va durer toujours
ce que tu te goures
fillette fillette
ce que tu te goures

les beaux jours s'en vont
les beaux jours de fête
soleils et planètes
tournent tous en rond
mais toi ma petite
tu marches tout droit
vers sque tu vois pas
très sournois s'approchent
la ride véloce
la pesante graisse
le menton triplé
le muscle avachi
allons cueille cueille
les roses les roses
roses de la vie
et que leurs pétales
soient la mer étale
de tous les bonheurs
allons cueille cueille
si tu le fais pas
ce que tu te goures
fillette fillette
ce que tu te goures

PAUVRE TYPE

Toto a un nez de chèvre et un pied de porc
Il porte des chaussettes
en bois d'allumette
et se peigne les cheveux
avec un coupe-papier qui a fait long feu
S'il s'habille les murs deviennent gris
S'il se lève le lit explose
S'il se lave l'eau s'ébroue
Il a toujours dans sa poche
un vide-poche

Pauvre type

Pour un Art Poétique

I

Un poème c'est bien peu de chose
à peine plus qu'un cyclone aux Antilles
qu'un typhon dans la mer de Chine
un tremblement de terre à Formose

Une inondation du Yang Tse Kiang
ça vous noie cent mille Chinois d'un seul coup
vlan
ça ne fait même pas le sujet d'un poème
Bien peu de chose

On s'amuse bien dans notre petit village
on va bâtir une nouvelle école
on va élire un nouveau maire et changer les jours
    de marché
on était au centre du monde on se trouve maintenant
    près du fleuve océan qui ronge l'horizon

Un poème c'est bien peu de chose

Pour un Art Poétique

III

Bien placés bien choisis
quelques mots font une poésie
les mots il suffit qu'on les aime
pour écrire un poème
on sait pas toujours ce qu'on dit
lorsque naît la poésie
faut ensuite rechercher le thème
pour intituler le poème
mais d'autres fois on pleure on rit
en écrivant la poésie
ça a toujours kékchose d'extrême
un poème

V

Bon dieu de bon dieu que j'ai envie d'écrire un
    petit poème
Tiens en voilà justement un qui passe
Petit petit petit
viens ici que je t'enfile
sur le fil du collier de mes autres poèmes
viens ici que je t'entube
dans le comprimé de mes œuvres complètes
viens ici que je t'enpapouète
et que je t'enrime
et que je t'enrythme
et que je t'enlyre
et que je t'enpégase
et que je t'enverse
et que je t'enprose

la vache
il a foutu le camp

Pour un Art Poétique

VI

L'encrier noir au clair de lune
l'encrier noir au clair de lune
au clair de la lune un encrier noir
au clair de la lune un encrier noir
au pauvre poète a prêté sa plume
au pauvre poète a prêté sa plume
il fait un peu frais ce soir
au clair de la lune un encrier noir
sur le papier blanc a couru la plume

la plume a couru zen petits traits noirs
une lune blanche un sombre encrier
sont les père et mère de ce nouveau-né
une lune blanche un sombre encrier

VII

Quand les poètes s'ennuient alors il leur ar-
Rive de prendre une plume et d'écrire un po-
Ème on comprend dans ces conditions que ça bar-
Be un peu quelque fois la poésie la po-
Ésie

Pour un Art Poétique

VIII

Ousqu'est mon registre à poèmes
moi qui voulais . . .
pas de papier pas de plume
plus de poème
me voici en face de rien
de rien du tout
du néant
ah que je me sens métaphysique
sans feu ni chandelle
pour la poétique

IX

Ce soir
si j'écrivais un poème
pour la postérité?

fichtre
la belle idée

je me sens sûr de moi
j'y vas
et

à
la
postérité
j'y dis merde et remerde
et reremerde

drôlement feintée
la postérité
qui attendait son poème

ah mais

Pour un Art Poétique

XI

Un train qui siffle dans la nuit
C'est un sujet de poésie
Un train qui siffle en Bohême
C'est là le sujet d'un poème

Un train qui siffle mélod-
Ieusement c'est pour une ode
Un train qui siffle comme un sansonnet
C'est bien un sujet de sonnet

Et un train qui siffle comme un hérisson
Ça fait tout un poème épique
Seul un train sifflant dans la nuit
Fait un sujet de poésie

«Sage renard aux yeux subtils»

Sage renard aux yeux subtils
serpent certain herbes fertiles
atouts des fleurs dans la prairie
l'oiseau filant entre les branches
le soleil dur l'eau qui sourit
la poule qui secoua ses manches...
....
... les plumes volent ô subtil
renard que le piège agile
pique: puis l'herbe qui s'écarte
recueille les sangs mélangés
de l'oiselle au col écarlate
et du chasseur assassiné!

L'ESPÈCE HUMAINE

L'espèce humaine m'a donné
le droit d'être mortel
le devoir d'être civilisé
la conscience humaine
deux yeux qui d'ailleurs ne fonctionnent pas très bien
le nez au milieu du visage
deux pieds deux mains
le langage
l'espèce humaine m'a donné
mon père et ma mère
peut-être des frères on ne sait
des cousins à pelletées
et des arrière-grands-pères
l'espèce humaine m'a donné
ses trois facultés
le sentiment l'intelligence et la volonté
chaque chose de façon modérée
l'espèce humaine m'a donné
trente-deux dents un cœur un foie
d'autres viscères et dix doigts
l'espèce humaine m'a donné
de quoi se dire satisfait

LES CHIENS D'ASNIÈRES

On enterre les chiens on enterre les chats
on enterre les chevaux on enterre les hommes
on enterre l'espoir on enterre la vie
on enterre l'amour — les amours
on enterre les amours — l'amour
on enterre en silence le silence
on enterre en paix — la paix
la paix — la paix la plus profonde
sous une couche de petits graviers multicolores
de coquilles Saint-Jacques et de fleurs multicolores

il y a une tombe pour tout
à condition d'attendre
il fait nuit il fait jour
à condition d'attendre
la Seine descend vers la mer
l'île immobile ne descend pas
la Seine remontera vers sa source
à condition d'attendre
et l'île naviguera vers le Havre de Grâce
à condition d'attendre

on enterre les chiens on enterre les chats
deux espèces qui ne s'aiment pas

LES À-PEU-PRÈS

À l'à peu près des cygnes
chante les canetons
à l'à peu près d'un pin
tinte deux clochetons

à l'à peu près d'un âne
se trémousse un currton
à l'à peu près d'un paon
susurre un hanneton

à l'à peu près d'un aulne
poussent fiers des oignons
à l'à peu près d'un on
passent bien trop de connes

à l'à peu près d'un poème
miaulent les crincrins
les crincrins critiques
et les tictics à crin

LE GAI RÉTAMEUR

Qui sait si l'on meurt
dit le rétameur
baisant la coquille d'une casserole ronde
car si la rumeur
prévient le r'ameur
alors je ne m'inquiéterai plus de rien au monde

L'étain coule mélancolique
le long du trottoir piétiné
il pleut dans cette boutique
ouverte à tous les vents désolés

Je ne pense pas
que le dit trépas
viendra m'étreindre dans ses deux bras de velours rouge
vit-on jamais ça
ce manque de tact
ce grossier rappel qu'ici-bas toute chose bouge

Partout la nuit s'illumine
et les éclairs dansent dans l'égout
si la clarté se dissémine
comment croire à la fin de tout

Qui sait si l'on meurt
dit le rétameur
baisant la coquille d'une casserole ronde
car si la rumeur
prévient le r'ameur
alors je ne m'inquiéterai plus de rien au monde

IDÉES

Les oiseaux bleus dans l'air sont verts dans la prairie
qui les entend les voit qui les voit les entend
leur aile déployée élargit leur patrie
mais à travers leur plume un feu toujours s'étend

Caméléons du ciel agiles que l'œil transperce
nuages qui vivants assument tour à tour
la forme d'une idée et puis l'idée adverse
protéens dont l'azur ne limite aucun tour

ils volent à travers la sublime excellence
des principes divins scellés sur l'horizon
les étoiles parfois dénotent leur présence
et les jeux de la lune au cours d'une saison

OMBRE D'UN DOUTE

Je mdemandd squ'on fait icigo
sur cette boule d'indigo
c'est pour la rime qu'on dit ça
et c'est pour la raison sans doute
que tout lmonde va sfairfoutre
en grand habit de tralala

on est là comme cornichons
susglobnaturellement rond
comment trouver d'autre épithète
de même qu'après l'agonie
quand on sait bien que c'est fini
faut dire qu'en fait il réquièste

les gens vont à droite et à goche
comme si y avait pas d'anicroche
car c'est la vie euh qui veut ça
et c'est la mort assurément
qui provoque ces enterrments
qu'on aperçoit ici et là

UN MILLION DE FAITS

Sur ma table repose un almanach Hachette
de mil neuf cent vingt-deux. Il fallut que j'achète
au prix de quatre francs cet étrange bouquin
que peu souvent on voit vêtu de maroquin
ou de cuir de Russie un jour que la pratique
m'obligeait à connaître un fait de statistique
concernant la culture admise désormais
de l'opium qu'aux Chinois imposent les Anglais
L'ouvrage se présente aux yeux sous une forme
agréable: il n'est point léger non plus qu'énorme
Il a plus de deux cents pages in-octavo
et moins de trois cents; on le vend couvert de veau
souple; on le dit impartial et documentaire
son érudition couvre toute la terre
Qui veut savoir comment se nomme du Japon
le ministre des Sports n'a qu'à prendre ce bon
livre afin d'y trouver à la page voulue
le renseignement puis cette phrase étant lue
il pourra reporter sa totale attention
sur le compte rendu qu'on fait de la tension
diplomatique entre URSS et pays balkaniques
dont le sol est truffé de pierres volcaniques
à ce qu'il me semblait. Mais en vain j'ai cherché
la géologie et j'en suis tout dégoûté